Honestly!*

Kelly Doudna

Consulting Editor, Diane Craig, M.A./Reading Specialist

Published by ABDO Publishing Company, 4940 Viking Drive, Edina, Minnesota 55435.

Credits
Edited by: Pam Price
Curriculum Coordinator: Nancy Tuminelly
Cover and Interior Design and Production: Mighty Media
Photo Credits: AbleStock, BananaStock Ltd., Hemera, Image 100, Image Source

Library of Congress Cataloging-in-Publication Data

Doudna, Kelly, 1963-
    Honestly! / Kelly Doudna.
      p. cm. -- (Character concepts)
    ISBN-13: 978-1-59928-735-5
    ISBN-10: 1-59928-735-8
    1. Honesty--Juvenile literature. I. Title.

    BJ1533.H7D68 2007
    179'.9--dc22

                                                                    2006032276

SandCastle™ books are created by a professional team of educators, reading specialists, and content developers around five essential components—phonemic awareness, phonics, vocabulary, text comprehension, and fluency—to assist young readers as they develop reading skills and strategies and increase their general knowledge. All books are written, reviewed, and leveled for guided reading, early reading intervention, and Accelerated Reader® programs for use in shared, guided, and independent reading and writing activities to support a balanced approach to literacy instruction.

Let Us Know

SandCastle would like to hear your stories about reading this book. What is your favorite page? Was there something hard that you needed help with? Share the ups and downs of learning to read. We want to hear from you! To get posted on the ABDO Publishing Company Web site, send us e-mail at:

sandcastle@abdopublishing.com

SandCastle Level: Transitional

Honestly!

Your character is a part of who you are. It is how you act when you go somewhere. It is how you get along with other people. It is even what you do when no one is looking!

You show character by being honest. You admit the truth, even if it's hard to do. You would never blame your little brother for something you did!

Grace broke a flowerpot.

She admits it to her dad.

Grace tells the truth.

Daniel snuck a cookie while no one was looking. He knows it was wrong to take the cookie, so he tells his mom what he did. Daniel tells the truth.

Ava doesn't want to help with chores. She pretends to be sick. But Ava knows that isn't being honest. So she decides to tell the truth.

Isabel's brother made fun of her dress. She is upset. She tells her brother how she really feels. She is honest.

Gavin tells his dad that he is going to the park. He says who will be with him. Gavin is honest.

Honestly!

James broke
the window
and now must
make a choice.
He can pretend
it didn't happen
or speak up
in a brave voice.

James thinks
for a minute
about which
path to take.
He wishes
it weren't so,
but the window
did break.

James goes
to his dad
and taps him
on the arm.
He says, "I wasn't
very careful,
and the window
came to harm."

James thinks
to himself,
"I'm glad I was
honest about the
broken window.
Now I feel good
from head to toe!"

Did You Know?

According to a popular but untrue story, President George Washington uttered the famous line, "I cannot tell a lie."

A television game show called *To Tell the Truth* had three contestants who claimed to be the same person. Panelists had to guess which one was telling the truth.

In movies and television shows, truth serum is a favorite way to get someone to spill the beans. In reality, truth serum produces unreliable results.

Glossary

admit – to say that something is so.

brave – having or showing courage.

chore – a regular job or task, such as cleaning your room.

pretend – to make believe.

sneak – to move, give, or take in a stealthy manner.

upset – being emotionally distressed.

About SandCastle™

A professional team of educators, reading specialists, and content developers created the SandCastle™ series to support young readers as they develop reading skills and strategies and increase their general knowledge. The SandCastle™ series has four levels that correspond to early literacy development in young children. The levels are provided to help teachers and parents select appropriate books for young readers.

Emerging Readers
(no flags)

Beginning Readers
(1 flag)

Transitional Readers
(2 flags)

Fluent Readers
(3 flags)

These levels are meant only as a guide. All levels are subject to change.

ABDO
Publishing Company

To see a complete list of SandCastle™ books and other nonfiction titles from ABDO Publishing Company, visit **www.abdopublishing.com** or contact us at: 4940 Viking Drive, Edina, Minnesota 55435 • 1-800-800-1312 • fax: 1-952-831-1632